Beyond the edge of sorrow
(Title)

Verses of love, loss and forever
(Subtitle)

Abdul Sadik
(Author)

Copyright page

Disclaimer

This book is a work of creativity and personal expression. The poems within are inspired by universal themes of love, loss, and healing, and are meant to evoke reflection and connection.

The content is not intended as professional advice or therapy. Readers are encouraged to interpret the poems in their own way, drawing upon their unique experiences and emotions. Any similarities to actual events, places, or persons—living or deceased—are purely coincidental unless explicitly stated.

Thank you for respecting the creative process behind this collection.

TABLE OF CONTENTS

INTRODUCTION

Life is a journey woven with moments of love, joy, loss, and remembrance. This book, 'Beyond the edge of sorrow;
VERSES OF LOVE, LOSs, AND FOREVER
is a heartfelt collection of poems dedicated to those tender moments that shape our hearts. Each piece reflects the beauty of connection, the ache of absence, and the enduring strength of love that

continues to shine even in the darkest hours.

Grief and love are two sides of the same coin, inseparable and eternal. Through words, we can explore the depth of these emotions, finding solace, comfort, and the courage to embrace the memories of those we hold dear. The poems within these pages serve as a gentle reminder that love never truly fades —it transforms, carrying us forward and filling the

empty spaces with light.

Whether you are seeking comfort, reflecting on a loss, or simply looking for a touch of beauty in your day, this book invites you to pause and connect with your heart. It is a quiet companion, offering its embrace to remind you that, even in grief, love remains constant— like stars in the night sky, forever present, guiding us with their glow.

The missing hug

I miss your hug, so warm, so tight,
That held me close through every night.
It made me feel safe, calm, and strong,
As though with you, nothing went wrong.

I try to wrap my arms around
The love you left; it can't be found.
But in my dreams, I see your face,
And feel the warmth of your embrace.

I close my eyes, and there you are,
Not gone, but near, not very far.
Your hug, like sunlight, lights my way,
And stays with me through every day.

Though you are not here, I still can feel
The hug you gave, so soft, so real.
It lives inside, where love is true,
Forever here, because of you.

And when I'm lonely, scared, or small,
I know your hug will catch my fall.
It's like a whisper in my ear,
That says, "I'm with you. I am here."

Forever in my heart

I hold you close, though you're not here,
In every thought, you feel so near.
Though time may take your voice away,
Your love is here, it's here to stay.

It lives inside my heart so small,
Like a candle bright that warms it all.
Though I can't see your smiling face,
I feel your love in every space.

Forever is a big, big word,
But your love's the truest thing I've heard.
It stays with me through night and day,
And never, ever fades away.

When I laugh, I think of you;
When I cry, your love shines through.
You've left a mark so deep, so real,
A part of you I'll always feel.

Though hands can't touch and eyes can't see,
Your love is here, it stays with me. And as I
grow and learn and start, You'll always live
inside my heart.

A Quiet tear

Sometimes I feel a tear,
Sneak slowly down my cheek.
It doesn't have a voice,
It doesn't even speak.

It hides in silence, soft and still,
Like a secret it won't tell.
It holds the words I cannot say,
And the love I keep so well.

Each tear remembers your kind smile,
Your laugh that filled the air.
It's a gentle whisper from my heart,
A way to show I care.

Though tears may fall like drops of rain,
I know that they will dry.
But memories of you, my dear,
Will always make me cry.

For every tear is love I hold,
A treasure deep and near.
Though grief feels heavy in my heart,
I send it with a tear.

Your Voice

I close my eyes and hear your song,
A melody soft, clear, and strong.
It carries me through every day,
Even though you've gone away.

Your voice is like a gentle breeze,
It floats and whispers through the trees.
It speaks of love, it speaks of care,
It's like you're here, though you're not there.

I try to sing it back to you,
A little hum, a note or two.
It feels like sharing, soft and sweet,
A way to make my heart complete.

Though silence sometimes fills the air,
Your voice is something I still share.
I carry it inside my heart,
It keeps us close, though we're apart.

And when I'm sad or feeling small,
Your voice will always catch my fall.
It's like a song that doesn't fade,
A gift of love you softly made.

The empty Chair

The chair you loved now sits alone,
Its arms are cold as silent stone.
No laughter rings, no stories flow,
Your warmth is gone, yet love won't go.

I sit beside it, close my eyes,
And picture you beneath the skies.
Your smile, your voice, still fill the air,
Though I can't see you sitting there.

The chair is more than just a seat,
It held the heart that made me complete.
Its emptiness is loud and wide,
A quiet ache I feel inside.

But when I sit and rest my hand,
I almost feel you understand.
The chair holds love that never fades,
A treasure of the times we made.

Though it is empty, it still speaks—
Of moments full, of days and weeks.
The chair reminds me you were here,
And keeps your memory crystal clear.

Sad and bright

My heart feels heavy, full of rain,
A quiet ache, a gentle pain.
It whispers softly, day and night,
Of moments sad and moments bright.

The sadness feels like waves at sea,
It rises strong and crashes me.
But then the love you left behind
Brings sunlight back into my mind.

It's strange to feel two things at once—
A heavy heart, a glowing chance.
The sadness says you're not around,
But love is here; it can't be drowned.

For every tear, a smile will bloom,
For every ache, a quiet room
Where love will stay and softly glow,
To tell me what I need to know.

That even when the skies feel grey,
Your love will never drift away.
It's sad and bright, all mixed in one,
Like rainy clouds that hold the sun.

Stars at night

When I see the stars at night,
I think of you and hold you tight.
Their twinkle feels like your kind eyes,
Bright and calm in endless skies.

The stars remind me you're still near,
A quiet glow that wipes my fear.
Though you are far, I feel your light,
It's soft and strong and always right.

Each star becomes a tiny hug,
A thread of love so tightly snug.
It shines above to guide my way,
And fills the dark with love each day.

Even when the night feels cold,
The stars tell stories I've been told.
They speak of you and all you gave,
Of love that's deep, of hearts so brave.

So when the sky is vast and wide,
I know you're there, you never hide.
You're in the stars, you shine for me,
A love that's endless as the sea.

Little bird

A little bird sang by my door,
Its voice was sweet, its song was sure.
It made me smile, it made me feel,
A warmth inside, so soft, so real.

But one day, it flew far away,
Its wings so light, its colors gray.
I watched it fade into the sky,
And all I could do was wonder why.

The tree feels quiet, empty now,
No song, no bird upon its bough.
But when the wind begins to sing,
I feel the flutter of its wing.

The little bird may not return,
But still its song in me will burn.
It taught me love, it taught me care,
It taught me life is always there.

So when I see the clouds above,
I think of it, and all its love.
The little bird is far, it's true,
But every song it sang was you.

Invisible hand

I feel your hand, though it's not there,
It brushes lightly through my hair.
It warms my shoulder, holds me tight,
A quiet touch that feels so right.

Your hand, once real, now feels like air,
A tender gift I sense with care.
It leads me when I feel unsure,
A guide, a promise strong and pure.

I hold my hand out to the sky,
And feel you take it, standing by.
Though I can't see, I know you're near,
Your hand brings comfort, calms my fear.

And in the moments I'm alone,
I feel your love, so softly shown.
It wraps around me, still and true,
A gift of strength, a part of you.

Invisible, yet always clear,
Your hand reminds me you are here.
Though gone, your touch will always stay,
A part of me, in every way.

Rain and love

The rain falls gently from the sky, Each
drop a tear for my goodbye. It lands on
flowers, soft and sweet, And makes the
ground beneath my feet.

Though rain can make the world seem gray,
It helps the colors find their way.
The flowers bloom, the leaves turn green,
A secret beauty, fresh and clean.

Grief feels like rain upon my face,
A steady stream I can't erase.
But just like rain, it helps me grow,
And teaches me what love can show.

For even when the skies are blue,
The love I feel will carry through.
It stays with me, both near and far,
A gentle light, a guiding star.

Rain falls, but soon the sun will glow,
And all the love I'll always know
Will fill my heart and make it shine,
Forever yours, forever mine.

A love that says

I thought that love could drift away,
Like shadows fading with the day.
But now I know it isn't true—
Love stays with me because of you.

It doesn't leave, it doesn't hide,
It lives within, so deep inside.
It whispers softly when I'm low,
"I'm here, my love. You'll always know."

Your love's a candle burning bright,
A steady glow that lights the night.
It's in my heart, it's in the air,
A quiet warmth that says you care.

Though time may pass and days may fade,
The love we shared will never trade.
It's here forever, always near,
A bond that's strong, a bond so clear.

So when I feel alone or small,
I know your love will catch it all.
It stays, it shines, it makes me see
That you'll be part of all I'll be.

A picture frame

I see your picture on the wall, A little smile,
so warm, so small. It takes me back to days
we knew, When life felt bright, when skies
were blue.

Your photo tells a story sweet,
Of love so full, of life complete.
It's like a window I can see,
To moments shared by you and me.

Though frames may fade and colors dim,
The heart inside will always brim.
Your photo holds the joy we made,
A light that time can never shade.

I touch the frame and close my eyes,
And feel your love beneath the skies.
It's more than just a picture there—
It's memories and love we share.

Though you are gone, the photo stays,
A piece of you through all my days.
And when I feel the world seems strange,
The picture holds what doesn't change.

Tiny Stars

Grief feels like tiny stars at night,
Each one a tear, each one a light.
They sparkle softly in the sky,
And whisper gently, "Don't ask why."

Each star is love that burns so deep,
A memory bright I'll always keep.
They twinkle softly, far yet near,
A sign of hope, a drop of cheer.

Though grief feels heavy, like a stone,
These tiny stars say, "You're not alone."
They hold the love that doesn't fade,
A glowing gift the heavens made.

And when I'm lost or filled with fear,
I look above and see them clear.
The stars remind me love won't die,
It simply moves into the sky.

So when the night feels cold and wide,
I know the stars are on my side.
They shine for me, they shine for you,
A bond so strong, so pure, so true.

Wishing for you

I close my eyes and make a wish, As
soft as bubbles in a dish. I wish for
you to be so near, To hear your
voice, to feel you here.

I wish for hugs, I wish for smiles,
For laughter shared across the miles.
I wish to see your face once more,
To feel the love I still adore.

But wishes float like leaves in air,
They drift and land, they're everywhere.
And though my wish may not come true,
It carries all my love to you.

For wishing is a secret way
To send you love across the day.
It's like a bridge that time can't break,
A glowing path my heart will take.

And when I wish upon a star,
I know you're close, not very far.
My wish becomes a part of me,
A dream of love that sets me free.

An ocean

Grief is like the ocean wide,
Its waves roll in, its feelings hide.
Sometimes it's calm, sometimes it roars,
It washes up on lonely shores.

The tide will rise, the tide will fall,
Its rhythm answers to no call.
But in its depths, so dark and true,
Are treasures there that come from you.

For every wave that crashes near,
It brings a memory soft and clear.
It holds the love we cannot lose,
A gift the ocean cannot refuse.

And though its waters may seem cold,
The warmth of love is pure and bold.
It carries me through every storm,
A quiet hand, a heart so warm.

Grief is like the sea, they say,
It doesn't leave, it doesn't stay.
It moves and shifts, it ebbs and flows,
And with it, love forever grows.

A Whisper

I heard your voice upon the breeze,
A soft hello among the trees.
It whispered gently in my ear,
"Be brave, my love, I'm always near."

The wind wrapped 'round me like a hug,
Its breath so warm, its pull so snug.
It held the words I long to hear,
It carried love so pure, so clear.

Though whispers fade and winds may go,
Your message lingers, soft and slow.
It tells me things I need to know,
That love stays bright, it will not go.

Your voice, though soft, is strong and true,
It lights my path, it pulls me through.
It's like a star upon the night,
A little spark, a steady light.

So when the breeze begins to play,
I'll close my eyes and drift away.
I'll hear your whisper, feel your care,
And know that you are always there.

A warm blanket

Grief feels like the coldest night, With shadows creeping out of sight. It wraps around, so tight and strong, And makes me feel that I don't belong. The chill it brings feels hard to bear, Like icy winds that fill the air. It whispers doubts, it hides the sun, And makes me think the warmth is done. But love is like a blanket warm, It shields me from the roughest storm. It wraps me tight and holds me near, And wipes away each lonely tear. The blanket isn't something seen; It's made of all the love you've been. It's made of hugs, of smiles, too, Of all the joy I found in you. So when the night feels dark and deep, Your love will help me rest and sleep. It keeps me safe, it holds me tight, And guides me gently to the light.

My secret wish

I see a star so high and bright,
It sparkles softly through the night.
I close my eyes and make a wish,
A tiny hope, a gentle kiss.

My wish is simple, quiet, true—
To spend one more sweet day with you.
To hear your laugh, to hold your hand,
To understand, to just...understand.

But wishes, like the stars, must fly,
Across the heavens, through the sky.
They travel far, they're never near,
But they carry love so strong, so clear.

And even if my wish won't show,
It plants a seed where love will grow.
It blooms inside, a secret way,
To bring you closer every day.

So each time I see a shining light,
I'll send my wish into the night.
And though the stars are far and wide,
You're always standing by my side.

A candle's glow

The world feels dark, the room is still,
The quietness feels sharp and chill.
But in the dark, I see a glow,
A candle's light, soft and slow.

The flame is small, it doesn't shout,
But chases all the shadows out.
Its golden warmth begins to spread,
It lights the path where I once tread.

This candle's flame is you, my dear,
It shines so bright, it keeps me near.
Though you are gone, the light remains,
To warm my heart through joy and pains.

And when the wind begins to blow,
The flame may flicker, but it won't go.
Its steady glow will light the way,
And turn my night into the day.

For love is like a candle's flame,
It burns forever, stays the same.
And even when the room feels bare,
Your light will always linger there.

A Flower for You

I pick a flower, soft and small,
The prettiest one of them all.
Its petals curl, its scent is sweet,
A treasure resting at my feet.

The flower makes me think of you,
Its colors bright, its heart so true.
It grows in sunlight, rain, and shade,
A symbol of the love we made.

I hold it gently in my hand,
And feel its beauty, understand.
That life is brief, like flowers, too,
But it's the love that carries through.

I place the flower by your name,
A quiet gift, a tiny flame.
It's not enough to say what's real,
But maybe it will help me heal.

For every flower, fresh or dried,
Is love that lives, not one that's died.
And when I see them bloom and grow,
I'll feel the love I always know.

Footprints in the Sand

I walk along the sandy shore,
The waves rush in, then leave once more.
The footprints follow where I stand,
A mark of life upon the sand.

But there's a space, an empty trail,
Where your sweet steps no longer sail.
I pause and wonder where you've gone,
Your path now silent, lost, withdrawn.

Yet as I watch the ocean blue,
I feel a presence soft and true.
Your footprints linger in my heart,
They're with me still, we're not apart.

The sand may shift, the waves may play,
But love's impression doesn't stray.
It holds the memories we've shared,
The love that shows you've always cared.

So though the sand may hide your steps,
The love you gave is what is kept.
And as I walk, I'll always find
Your footprints linger in my mind.

Shadows and light

Shadows fall, they stretch and creep,
They settle in where silence sleeps.
They make the world feel cold and small,
A lonely, endless, empty hall.

But even shadows have their place,
They're not just darkness; they're a space.
Where light can grow and gently shine,
A quiet love, a bright design.

For grief is shadowed by the past,
But love shines through, a light that lasts.
It turns the dark to something new,
A balance soft, a glowing hue.

And when the night feels still and long,
Your love will sing its steady song.
A light that doesn't fade away,
A guide to bring me through the day.

Shadows and light walk hand in hand,
Together they help me understand.
That even when the skies feel gray,
Love always finds a brighter way.

A Broken Clock

The clock sits quiet, its hands don't move,
Its ticking rhythm cannot prove
The passing time, the days ahead,
It only whispers what is dead.

It feels like time has stopped for me,
Each moment locked in memory.
The seconds stretch, the minutes freeze,
My heart is still, it feels no ease.

But even clocks that break and stay
Still hold the time of yesterday.
They show the moments we held dear,
The love we made, the joy so clear.

Though time has paused, I feel its hand,
It carries me, helps me withstand.
For every hour you were near
Lives on inside, so bright, so clear.

A broken clock reminds me, too,
That time is love, and love is you.
Though hands don't move, the love is there,
Forever ticking in the air.

The last hug

I close my eyes and hold you tight,
A hug that lingers through the night.
I feel your warmth, your steady heart,
As if we'll never drift apart.

The last hug stays inside my chest,
A memory strong, my softest rest.
Its arms are wide, they hold me still,
A love so deep, it always will.

Though you are gone, the hug remains,
It wraps me up through joy and pains.
It's like a shield, a comfort sweet,
A place where love and sorrow meet.

When life feels lonely, cold, and bare,
I feel your hug still resting there.
It whispers, "I'm not far away,
I'm here, my love, each passing day."

The last hug isn't truly last,
It bridges now and all the past.
And every time my arms reach wide,
I feel you standing by my side.

A Feather Falls

A feather drifts down from the sky,
It dances soft, it floats so high.
It lands so gently, light as air,
A quiet gift that says you care.

The feather feels like you to me,
A sign from somewhere I can't see.
It whispers softly, "I'm still here,
I haven't gone, I'm always near."

Its touch is light, but strong enough,
To remind me of your endless love.
It brings me peace, it lifts my heart,
A way to feel we're not apart.

Though feathers fall, they never break,
They carry all the love they make.
And every time I see one glide,
I feel your presence by my side.

A feather falls, a gift of you,
A tiny hope, a sign so true.
It tells me love is everywhere,
A bond that lives beyond the air.

A Quiet Place

There is a place I go to hide,
A space where grief and love collide.
It's calm and still, it holds me near,
A quiet place where you appear.

The trees are tall, the grass is green,
The world feels soft, the air serene.
Your voice is there, your hand is, too,
It feels like home, a place for you.

In this small spot, the pain feels less,
A secret world of love and rest.
It's where my heart can softly mend,
A place where sorrow turns to friend.

The quiet place is always mine,
It's filled with love, a space divine.
And though it lives inside my head,
It carries all the words you said.

So when the world feels loud and tough,
The quiet place will be enough.
It keeps you close, it helps me see,
That love lives on inside of me.

A Cup of Tea

I hold a cup of tea so warm,
It soothes my heart, it keeps me calm.
Its steam floats gently through the air,
A quiet hug that says, "I care."

The tea reminds me of your love,
A simple gift, so full, so true.
Its warmth is soft, its taste is sweet,
A memory I'll always meet.

I sit and sip, and time slows down,
The world stops spinning all around.
This little cup is something small,
But it contains the love of all.

It holds the talks we used to share,
The laughter light, the moments rare.
Though you are gone, the tea remains,
A way to feel your warmth again.

Each sip I take brings peace and light,
A gentle glow to guide the night.
A cup of tea, so simple, true,
Holds all the love I feel for you.

Echoes

I call your name into the air,
It echoes back as if you're there.
The sound is soft, it fades away,
But leaves a mark that's here to stay.

The echoes feel like love's reply,
A message whispered through the sky.
They tell me, "I am here, don't fear,
You'll always feel my presence near."

Though echoes fade and sound may die,
They linger quietly nearby.
They carry all the love we made,
A bond that time can't ever fade.

Each word I speak, each name I say,
Returns to me in some sweet way.
It's like the air is full of you,
A love that's strong, a love so true.

So when I miss your voice and care,
I call your name into the air.
The echoes bring your love to me,
A song that's endless as the sea.

The moon's Face

The moon shines softly in the night,
Its face so calm, its glow so bright.
I look to it and think of you,
Its light is strong, its heart is true.

The moon reminds me of your care,
A quiet comfort always there.
It watches over all I do,
A steady friend to pull me through.

Its glow is soft, its pull is kind,
It helps me find some peace of mind.
And though it's far, it feels so near,
A presence strong, a love so clear.

Each night, it rises, bold and sure,
Its light a gift that will endure.
And as I watch it from my place,
I feel your love within its face.

The moon is constant, never gone,
A symbol that your love lives on.
So when I see its silver hue,
I know it's shining just for you.

A garden grows

Grief feels like an empty space, A hollow garden, a quiet place. No flowers bloom, no birds take flight, Just silent earth in shadowed light.

But love's a seed within the ground,
It waits for time to come around.
And when the rain begins to fall,
It whispers softly, "I'm here, that's all."

The garden slowly starts to grow,
A little sprout, a gentle glow.
The love you left begins to bloom,
It fills my heart, it lights the room.

Though grief still lingers in the air,
It mixes with the love we share.
The flowers bloom despite the pain,
A garden born from tears and rain.

So when I walk this garden wide,
I feel your love still by my side.
Each petal, leaf, and stem I see
Holds all the love you gave to me.

The light inside

When the world feels dark and gray,
And hope seems far, so far away,
I close my eyes and look within,
To find the love where you have been.

Your voice, your smile, your loving care,
Still live inside me, everywhere.
They light a candle in my chest,
A flame of love, my place of rest.

Grief can try to steal the glow,
To dim the love I've come to know.
But love is stronger, it won't fade,
It shines through every tear I've made.

The light inside is soft but strong,
It carries me when days feel wrong.
It holds your warmth, it holds your hand,
A quiet glow I understand.

So when the shadows feel too near,
I trust the light, so bright and clear.
It's you, it's love, it's all we've shared,
A bond unbroken, deeply cared.

A river runs

Grief is like a river wide,
Its waters strong, its currents hide.
It carries pain, it pulls me through,
Yet in its waves, I still find you.

The river flows, it doesn't rest,
It tests my heart, it fills my chest.
But every ripple, every crest,
Carries love I've been blessed.

Sometimes the waters rush and roar,
They crash against my spirit's shore.
But when the river runs so still,
I feel your love, I always will.

The river isn't just my grief,
It holds my hope, it brings relief.
For though it's deep, it carries care,
A way to feel you're always there.

So when I float or when I drown,
Your love will lift me, pull me down.
Grief may run, but love is wide,
A steady river by my side.

A tree stands

There's a tree that stands so tall,
It weathers storms, it catches fall.
Its roots are deep, its branches strong,
It holds my heart when things go wrong.

This tree reminds me of your love,
A gift that stretches far above.
It shelters me through wind and rain,
A place of peace, a cure for pain.

Though grief may try to bend its boughs,
The tree still stands, it won't allow
The storms of sorrow to take its place,
Its love remains, a quiet grace.

Each leaf that falls, each bud that grows,
Is proof of all the love it shows.
And though the seasons come and go,
Its heart beats steady, soft and slow.

The tree of love is always there,
Its roots so strong, its branches care.
And when I stand beneath its shade,
I know your love will never fade.

A quilt of love

Grief feels like a heavy night,
A blanket dark, a loss of light.
But love is like a patchwork quilt,
Of memories warm, of joy we built.

Each square is stitched with laughter sweet,
With moments shared, with hearts that meet.
The colors bright, the fabric strong,
A quilt that's kept me safe so long.

When grief feels cold, I hold it tight,
This quilt of love, this source of light.
It wraps me up, it keeps me near,
To all the love I still hold dear.

The stitches hold though time may pass,
The quilt won't fade, it will outlast.
It's made of you, of all you gave,
A love that's deep, a bond that's brave.

So when the nights feel dark and bare,
I pull this quilt around and care.
It's not goodbye, it's not the end,
Your love's my quilt, my constant friend.

A song remains

I hear your song upon the breeze,
A melody that soothes and frees.
Its notes are soft, its rhythm kind,
A tune that lingers in my mind.

The song reminds me of your care,
A voice that's here, a love that's there.
Though grief may try to hush the sound,
Your song of love is all around.

It plays within the quiet air,
It hums a tune beyond despair.
Its harmony is strong and true,
It holds the love I feel for you.

And when I sing, I find my voice,
A way to grieve, a way to rejoice.
The song becomes a part of me,
A bond of love, a melody.

Though time may fade and words may
end, Your song of love will still ascend.
It lives in me, it lives in light, A song
that carries through the night.

A letter to you

I write this letter, pen in hand,
Hoping you'll somehow understand.
The words I write are full of care,
Though you're not here, you're everywhere.

I tell you how my days go by,
How some are bright, and some I cry.
I tell you all I wish you'd see,
The little things that mean so much to me.

This letter feels like you're still near,
Like I can whisper, and you'll hear.
I fold it gently, hold it tight,
As if it brings your love to light.

Though you won't read the words I send,
They help my broken heart to mend.
Each letter's like a bridge of care,
A way to feel you're always there.

So I'll keep writing, line by line,
These letters to the love of mine.
Though grief is strong, love's stronger still,
A quiet bond that time can't kill.

The ocean knows

The ocean waves crash loud and clear,
They speak of things I cannot hear.
They tell of love, they tell of loss,
Of treasures found and tempests tossed.

The ocean knows the pain I keep,
It hides it in its waters deep.
Each wave that rises, every tide,
Carries the tears I've tried to hide.

But love is in the ocean, too,
In every drop, in every blue.
It holds the memories we made,
The laughter bright, the love that stayed.

The ocean whispers, soft and slow,
That grief will come, but love will grow.
And even when the storm feels wild,
Love finds a way, so calm and mild.

So when I watch the ocean's dance,
I feel your love in every glance.
The waves may crash, the winds may blow,
But love will linger, ebb, and flow.

A star that shines

I see a star up in the sky,
It twinkles softly, way up high.
Its light feels gentle, calm, and true,
It shines because of love and you.

The star reminds me of your care,
A light that's constant, always there.
Though grief may try to dim its glow,
Your love shines brighter than I know.

When nights feel dark and filled with fear,
I look to see your star appear.
It tells me that I'm not alone,
Your love's a light that's always shown.

And when I close my eyes to dream,
The star still sparkles, soft and clean.
It's you, it's love, it's all you gave,
A light that time could never shave.

So every night, I raise my gaze,
To see your love in starry rays.
Though grief may weigh my heart each day,
Your light will guide me on my way.

A whisper in the wind

The wind blows softly through the air,
It carries whispers everywhere.
I close my eyes, I listen near,
And in the breeze, your voice is clear.

"Don't be afraid," it seems to say,
"I'm with you now, I'll always stay.
Though you can't see me, I'm still here,
In every wind, in every tear."

The wind becomes a hug, a kiss,
A way to feel the love I miss.
It dances through the trees and skies,
A silent comfort where it lies.

Though grief may try to take its place,
The wind brings whispers, soft with grace.
It carries you in every sound,
A love that's deep, a bond profound.

So when the wind begins to play,
I'll feel your love, I'll hear you say:
"I'm here, I'm near, I never go,
In every breeze, in every flow."

The colours of love

Grief feels like gray, a cloudy hue,
A world that's quiet, cold, and blue.
But love brings color, bright and warm,
It paints my heart through every storm.

The red of laughter, bold and sweet,
The yellow joy of when we'd meet.
The green of peace you always gave,
The purple courage, strong and brave.

Each color lingers, doesn't fade,
It's in the love that we have made.
Though grief may try to dull the light,
Your colors shine, so strong, so bright.

I carry them within my chest,
A rainbow glowing, love's the rest.
And even when the gray appears,
Your colors soothe my deepest fears.

So when I see the world in gray,
I know your love will find a way.
To paint my life in hues so true,
A masterpiece of me and you.

A lantern in the dark

Grief feels like a long, dark night,
With no clear path, with no soft light.
But love's a lantern in my hand,
It helps me see, it helps me stand.

Its glow is warm, its flame is bright,
It carries hope through endless night.
Though shadows creep, though fear may rise,
The lantern burns, it never dies.

This lantern holds the love we shared,
The quiet moments, the way you cared.
It guides me through the darkest days,
With memories lighting all the ways.

Though grief may try to steal its flame,
Love keeps it strong, it stays the same.
And when I feel I've lost my way,
The lantern shows me where to stay.

So I will hold it, near and tight,
This lantern burning through the night.
It's you, it's love, it's all we've been,
A light that shines forever within.

The path we walked

I walk a path we used to tread,
Your hand in mine, our love ahead.
The trail was bright, the sun was high,
A journey shared, just you and I.

But now the path feels cold and bare,
I look behind, but you're not there.
Each step I take feels steep, unkind,
As grief walks close, not far behind.

Yet on this path, I feel you still,
Your strength, your love, your gentle will.
It's in the wind, the trees, the sky,
A quiet voice that says, "Don't cry."

The path is hard, but I'll go on,
Your love's the guide that leads me strong.
It shows me beauty, joy, and grace,
A way to find your sweet embrace.

So though I walk this path alone,
Your love is here, it's always shown.
Each step I take, I know you're near,
A steady presence, soft and clear.

A memory's touch

Your memory feels like a gentle hand,
It reaches out, it helps me stand.
Though I can't see you, touch your face,
Your love still holds a quiet space.

Each memory's like a sweet embrace,
A piece of you that time won't erase.
They comfort me when days feel long,
A silent strength that keeps me strong.

I see your smile, I hear your laugh,
A guiding light along my path.
Though grief may try to break me down,
Your memory lifts, it won't let me drown.

Each moment shared, each time we'd talk,
Is love that helps my spirit walk.
It's in the air, it's in my heart,
A gift from you that won't depart.

So when the world feels rough and bare,
I find your memory everywhere.
It's love, it's warmth, it's all we knew,
A touch that says, "I'm here with you."

Love is still here

I thought love would fade when you went away,
That the light in my heart would grow dim and gray.
But love doesn't vanish; it lingers and grows,
It's in the sun, the rain, and the rose.

It's in the quiet, the whisper of trees,
In the soft, steady hum of the evening breeze.
Though grief tries to tell me love's lost in the pain,
Your love shows me sunshine after the rain.

Each memory we made, each moment we shared,
Is proof that your love has always cared.
Though I can't hold your hand, see your face,
Your love fills the emptiest space.

Grief may visit, it may stay awhile,
But your love turns tears into a gentle smile.
It's not the end, though you're not near,
Because love remains—it's always here.

The moon remembers

The moon remembers the nights we knew,
When we'd watch the stars, just me and you.
Its silver light, so soft and still,
Feels like your touch, your gentle will.

Though grief now paints the nights in gray,
The moon reminds me you're not far away.
Its glow speaks softly, a quiet song,
Saying love endures, forever strong.

Each phase of the moon, full or thin,
Carries the love we've always been.
Even in shadow, its light remains,
A promise of love that grief can't restrain.

So I look to the moon when I feel lost,
When life feels heavy with grief's cost.
It whispers back, "I'm here, my dear,
In the light of love, always near."

A house of love

Grief feels like an empty home,
A house where I wander alone.
The rooms are quiet, the halls are bare,
But love is still living everywhere.

It's in the chair where you used to sit,
The table where we'd talk and knit.
It's in the walls, the floors, the air,
A quiet presence that says, "I'm there."

Though loss has tried to close the door,
Love's still alive within this floor.
It lingers in the smallest place,
In every memory, every trace.

This house may echo with my tears,
But love fills up the empty years.
It's not just grief—it's love I find,
A house of you, still kind and kind.

The heart
knows

Grief tries to tell my heart, "You're alone." But
my heart whispers back, "I've known. Love
isn't something that fades with time, It grows
like a tree, it always climbs."

Your love is the roots, the sturdy ground, The trunk
that holds when life spins around. Though branches
may bend, though leaves may fall, Your love keeps
growing through it all.

My heart carries you, every beat,
In the joy, the pain, the incomplete.
It knows you're here, though I can't see,
Your love a song, a melody.

Grief may visit, it may stay near,
But my heart knows love is clear.
It beats for you, it holds your name,
A bond unbroken, always the same.

A rainbow after rain

Tears fall like rain, heavy and cold,
Grief wraps me tight in its heavy fold.
But just as the storm begins to wane,
Love brings a rainbow after the rain.

Each color speaks of times we knew,
The laughter, the dreams, the love so true.
The red of passion, the yellow of cheer,
The green of hope that keeps you near.

Though grief may cloud the brightest sky,
Your love finds a way, it doesn't die.
The rainbow arches, bright and clear,
A promise that love will always appear.

So when the storm feels too much to bear,
I look to the sky and find you there.
Grief may rain, but love will stay,
A rainbow shining day by day.

In every Sunshine

Each morning brings the light of day,
A gentle warmth, a golden ray.
Though grief tries to keep the night,
Love always returns with the morning light

The sunrise feels like your embrace,
Its glow a memory I can't replace.
It reminds me that you're never gone,
You're in the dawn, in every song.

Though shadows linger, though tears may fa
The sunrise comes to answer them all.
It whispers softly, "Love is here,
In every beam, in every tear."

So I wake each day with you in mind,
Your love a light so warm, so kind.
Grief may visit, but love will rise,
In every sunrise, in every sky.

The echo of us

Grief is an echo, soft and low,
A shadowed sound where memories grow.
But love is the echo that answers back,
A steady rhythm when things feel black.

I hear your laughter in the breeze,
Your voice in whispers among the trees.
Though the echo fades, it doesn't end,
It loops and lingers, my closest friend.

Each sound reminds me of your care,
A love that's constant, always there.
Grief may try to fill the space,
But love returns with its quiet grace.

So when the echo calls my name,
I answer back—it's not the same.
But in its rhythm, soft and true,
I hear the love I found in you.

The bridge of memories

Grief feels like a broken road,
A path too heavy, a crushing load.
But memories build a bridge so wide,
A way to reach the other side.

Each laugh, each tear, each time we shared
Becomes a plank so strong, so cared.
Though grief may try to tear it down,
The bridge of love will hold its ground.

I walk that bridge when nights feel long,
I hear your voice, I feel your song.
It carries me through storm and rain,
A bond of love that will remain.

Though the road ahead may twist and bend
This bridge reminds me love won't end.
It's there to guide, to keep me true,
A path that always leads to you.

A fire that warms

Grief feels cold, a wintry night,
But love's a fire that burns so bright.
Its warmth is steady, its flame is clear,
It keeps me safe, it keeps you near.

The fire crackles, it softly glows,
A warmth that only true love knows.
Though loss may try to snuff it out,
The fire fights back, it shouts, it shouts.

It says, "I'm here, I won't let go,
My warmth is yours, you need to know."
And when the night feels dark and long,
The fire burns bright, it stays so strong.

Your love's the fire that lights my way,
Through every night, through every day.
Grief may chill, but love remains,
A steady fire in life's domains.

The Garden of us

Grief feels like weeds in a garden of dream
Tangled and heavy, bursting at seams.
But love is the seed that quietly grows,
Through cracks and shadows, it always show

The flowers we planted, the moments we ma
Bloom in my heart and never fade.
Though grief may darken the soil today,
Your love is the sun that lights my way.

Each petal whispers a memory sweet,
Each stem stands tall where we used to me
The garden lives, though you're not near,
It holds our love, so bright, so clear.

Even in grief, the blooms remain,
A gift of love through joy and pain.
The garden of us will always thrive,
A symbol that love keeps dreams alive.

A river between

Grief is a river, wild and deep,
It carries my tears, it steals my sleep.
But love is the shore, calm and wide,
A place of comfort on the other side.

The water flows with memories past,
Moments of joy that couldn't last.
Yet on the shore, your voice I hear,
Saying, "I'm with you, always near."

The current is strong, but I hold tight,
To the love that guides me through the night.
Though I can't cross to where you stand,
I feel your touch, a gentle hand.

Grief may surge, but love will stay,
A constant light to show the way.
The river between will never divide,
For love's the bridge where hearts collide.

The star you became

When you left, the night grew dark,
Grief took hold, left no spark.
But then I saw a star above,
It felt like you, shining love.

Its glow was steady, soft and true,
A quiet light that reminded me of you.
Even in sadness, I could see,
Your love still watches over me.

The star became my guide at night,
A beacon of hope, a calming light.
Though grief is here, it cannot hide,
The warmth of love you left inside.

Now when I look at the sky so vast,
I see your love—it will always last.
You are a star that will never fade,
A piece of light that grief can't shade.

The blanket of love

Grief feels cold, like a winter frost,
A chilling reminder of what I've lost.
But love is a blanket, soft and warm,
A shelter that shields me from the storm.

It wraps me close when nights are long,
Whispering comfort, keeping me strong.
Though tears may fall and sorrow stays,
Love's embrace lights brighter days.

Each thread is woven with times we knew,
Laughter, kindness, a bond so true.
Even when grief pulls me apart,
The blanket of love protects my heart.

So in the cold, when grief is near,
I feel your warmth, your presence clear.
Your love remains, a steady flame,
A comfort that keeps me whole again.

The clock stopped

When you left, time seemed to pause,
Grief stood still without a cause.
But love reminds me life goes on,
Even though you're truly gone.

Each tick of the clock feels bittersweet,
A reminder of days we'll never meet.
Yet love whispers, "Hold on tight,
Memories will guide you through the night."

Time moves slowly, but love is strong,
It keeps me steady, where I belong.
Though grief may linger, love will grow,
A constant force I've come to know.

The clock may tick, but love's not bound,
It lives beyond time, profound.
So I let the minutes move their way,
Knowing love is here to stay.

The bridge of light

Grief feels like a heavy cloud,
Silent, dark, a shadowed shroud.
But love is the light that breaks right through,
A golden path that leads to you.

Each step I take, though slow, unsure,
Love whispers softly, "You'll endure."
It builds a bridge from heart to heart,
Even when we're worlds apart.

The light shines bright in memories sweet,
In the songs you sang, in the love we'd meet.
Though grief tries hard to dim the glow,
Love stands firm, it will not go.

This bridge of light keeps you near,
A bond unbroken, strong and clear.
Though clouds may gather, love will stay,
A guiding bridge to brighter days.

Conclusion

As you turn the final page of this collection, I hope you carry with you the quiet strength that love and memory offer, even in the face of loss. These poems are not just words on a page; they are whispers of comfort, reminders that grief, though heavy, is not the end. Love persists, shifting and transforming, lighting the path through darkened times.

The journey through these verses may have touched something deep within you—memories, emotions, or silent spaces where healing begins. Know that even in moments of sorrow, you are not alone. The love we hold, the ones we've lost, and the connections we cherish remain with us in ways we often cannot see, but always feel.

Thank you for reading, for allowing these words to walk alongside you. May you find peace, comfort, and the courage to hold on to the love that lives within and around you, forever.

THANK YOU